Poems by
Jonathan Schkade

ICKY STICKY, HAIRY SCARY

ART BY
Tuesday Mourning

BIBLE STORIES

CONCORDIA PUBLISHING HOUSE • SAINT LOUIS

For Daniel, Josh, and Nathan

And for every kid who's ever said, **"Ew, gross!"**
and then smiled

Special thanks to Joan Tietz, whose creative input
helped to inspire this book.

Published by Concordia Publishing House
3558 S. Jefferson Avenue, St. Louis, MO 63118-3968
1-800-325-3040 • www.cph.org

Text © 2011 Jonathan Schkade
Illustrations © Concordia Publishing House

Manufactured in the United States of America

1 2 3 4 5 6 7 8 9 10   20 19 18 17 16 15 14 13 12 11

Want more icky sticky, hairy scary stuff? You do? (Really?!)

Then go to **www.cph.org/ickysticky** for fun activities.

DANGER!

Read at your own risk!!!

Silly "Icky Sticky" stories are waiting to slime you! Terrifying "Hairy Scary" stories have sharpened their claws and are eager to pounce!

The truly weird part?
These stories are all from the Bible, God's own Word.

But don't think this means they're tidy and safe. Oh, no. These stories are messy and dangerous and filled with foolish, strange, awful, and lovable people. They're filled with people like you and me. Best of all, though, they show that God loves us and is willing to sink down in the disgusting muck with us to lift us up and set us free.

So put on your apron and goggles! Get your helmet and shield! It's time to dig in to some Icky Sticky, Hairy Scary Bible Stories!

READ ON, IF YOU DARE!

icky sticky

hairy scary

icky sticky

A COW-EAT-COW WORLD

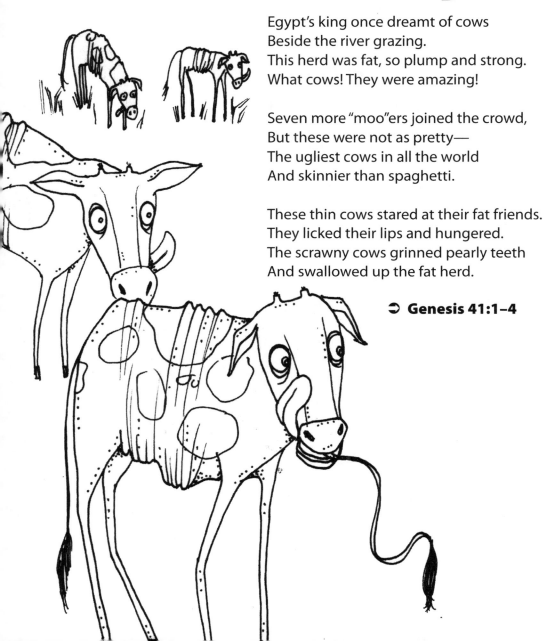

Egypt's king once dreamt of cows
Beside the river grazing.
This herd was fat, so plump and strong.
What cows! They were amazing!

Seven more "moo"ers joined the crowd,
But these were not as pretty—
The ugliest cows in all the world
And skinnier than spaghetti.

These thin cows stared at their fat friends.
They licked their lips and hungered.
The scrawny cows grinned pearly teeth
And swallowed up the fat herd.

➲ **Genesis 41:1–4**

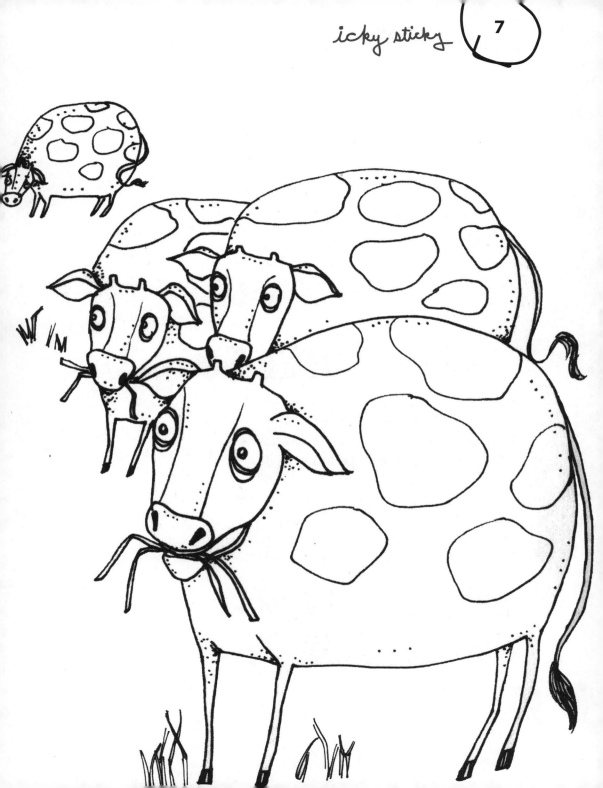

icky sticky

DEATH BY WORMS

Herod the king was a very proud man
Who doubted that Jesus had risen.
He'd ordered the killing of John's brother James
And tried to keep Peter in prison.

One day, Herod stood to make a long speech,
Wearing clothes with fancy gold trim.
After saying big words, he sat on his throne,
While the crowd shouted praises to him.

They called him a god, but he did not blush—
Herod actually thought he deserved it.
So at once God's angel struck the king down,
And he was eaten by worms and digested.

➲ **Acts 12:21–23**

LOSS, PAIN, AND ROTTEN FRIENDS

Faithful, rich, proud daddy Job
Was God's servant, true and deep.
He had three girls and seven sons
And donkeys, camels, sheep.

Job had so much and was so good
It came as quite a shock
When Satan took Job's wealth away,
Each camel, ox, and flock.

Worst of all, when Job was broke,
A party tent collapsed
And killed Job's daughters and his sons,
But Job's faith never lapsed.

Job tore his robes and shaved his head
And said, "Oh, woe is me!"
Such nasty sores covered his skin
He scraped with pottery.

His wife, who should have helped him out,
Just said, "Curse God and die."
But Job said, "God deserves our praise
Even when gifts run dry."

While Job was suffering, his three friends
Were supposed to soothe his pain.
Instead they said, "It's your fault, Job.
You must deserve the blame."

Then his friends said, "You're a worm,
A sinner, and a fink."
Finally, God said, "Job's My guy,
And, as friends, you three stink."

"Job," said God, "pray for these fools,
And for your sake, they'll live.
And then way more than what you lost,
I'll gladly to you give."

⮑ **The Book of Job**

icky sticky

HERE'S SPIT IN YOUR EYE

Jesus traveled place to place
Comforting and healing
The sick, the poor, the deaf, the lame—
All those who pain were feeling.

Now in one town, some people brought
To Jesus one quite blind,
Who hoped that with the Master's help
True vision he would find.

So Jesus spat on this man's eyes,
Touched them, and asked, "You see?"
The man said, "I see people here.
They look like walking trees."

Then Jesus touched his eyes again,
And full sight was restored.
The man once blind saw clearly now,
Thanks to his gracious Lord.

➲ **Mark 8:22–25**

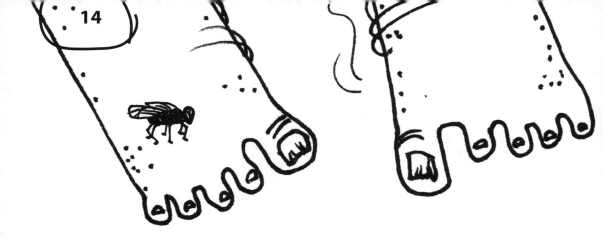

STINKY FEET

As the disciples were eating a meal
With Jesus, their great Lord and Teacher,
Jesus Himself stood up in their midst
To give a lesson to each here.

He moved from the table, stripped off His shirt,
Wrapped a towel 'round His waist.
With a tub full of water, He went one-by-one
To where His friends' feet were placed.

Their feet were real stinky and covered with dust
From roads full of dirt and manure.
They smelled of sweat from the work of the day—
It was almost as bad as a sewer.

But Jesus went to them, no matter how dirty,
And gently washed clean their feet.
He rinsed them with water and dried with His towel,
Then moved on to Simon, called Pete.

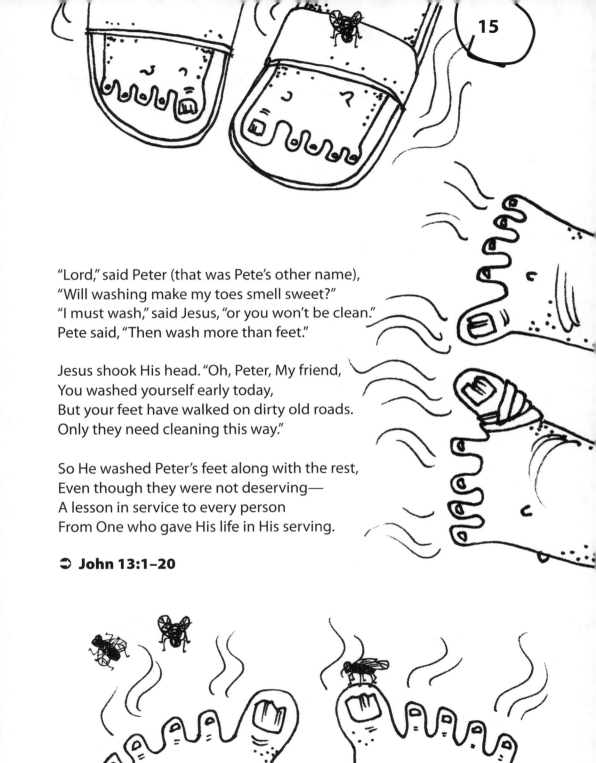

"Lord," said Peter (that was Pete's other name),
"Will washing make my toes smell sweet?"
"I must wash," said Jesus, "or you won't be clean."
Pete said, "Then wash more than feet."

Jesus shook His head. "Oh, Peter, My friend,
You washed yourself early today,
But your feet have walked on dirty old roads.
Only they need cleaning this way."

So He washed Peter's feet along with the rest,
Even though they were not deserving—
A lesson in service to every person
From One who gave His life in His serving.

⊃ **John 13:1–20**

A LOT TO SWALLOW

The Word of the Lord once came to Jonah,
A prophet whom God Himself chose:
"To Nineveh go, and tell them their sin,
And how it before My eyes rose."

But Jonah disliked the Ninevite people
And feared that God would show pity.
So he boarded a boat that was heading away
From that great and terrible city.

Quite soon mighty waves pushed hard at the boat,
And water poured over the deck.
The sailors were sure that they would all die,
Sunk and drowned in a nasty shipwreck.

Then Jonah woke up—he'd been taking a nap!—
And told them he'd angered the Lord.
He said that to bring this storm to an end,
They'd have to throw him overboard.

The men on the ship didn't like that idea,
So to land they tried hard to row.
The storm, though, got worse, and soon they gave in,
Tossing Jonah with one big heave-ho.

The storm disappeared, but was Jonah dead?
Not quite, for God had a plan.
A huge fish God sent gulped up Jonah whole—
A belly of mushed food and man.

Now normally fish can smell not so good,
And from inside they stink twice as bad.
But Jonah was grateful just to be alive
As he prayed to his heavenly Dad.

After three days with Jonah in its stomach,
The great fish barfed him upon land.
Slimed but alive, Jonah went on his way
To do as God all along planned.

➲ **Jonah 1:1–3:3**

THE PLANT, THE WORM, AND THE WHINY PROPHET

In Nineveh town, Jonah finally arrived
To proclaim God's word of great dread.
Through markets and streets, Jonah proudly announced,
"In forty days, you'll all be dead!"

Though the Ninevite people had done awful things,
Their king said, "Let's no more be bad!
We'll put ash on our heads and wear itchy clothes,
And no food or drink will be had."

When God saw them turning away from their sin,
True pity He felt in His heart.
God chose not to kill them, which seems like the end,
But then Jonah's whining did start.

"I hate all those people," said Jonah to God,
"And I knew all along You'd forgive.
Why do You think I at first ran away?
These sinners don't deserve to live!"

"You're being a jerk," God basically said,
But Jonah just pouted, still red.
He set up a tent a bit outside town
And hoped God would smite them all dead.

Then God made a plant grow tall and give shade
To keep Jonah's big head quite cool.
So Jonah was glad because this plant was great,
And he said, "Yo, planty, you rule!"

But God had a lesson for Jonah, so He
Sent a worm to eat up the plant.
When the sun made Jonah both dizzy and hot,
"I might as well die" was his rant.

"What is your problem?" said God
   unto him.
"You cry since you lost your shade.
Yet for all of those people and all
   of their cows
You've not any pity displayed."

⮑ **Jonah 3:4–4:11**

EXTRA CRUNCH IN THE LUNCH

When time was nearing
For Jesus to teach,
Our God sent before Him
Another to preach.

His name was called John.
In the wilds he dwelt,
In camel-hair clothing
Held tight by a belt.

And while odd John waited,
He baptized the crowd.
Eating honey and bugs,
On locusts he chowed.

Much more, John announced,
"Repent and prepare,"
For Jesus, who's greater,
Would quite soon appear.

➲ **Mark 1:2–8**

Just as dead flies make perfume stink, so small sins can mess up all your smart plans.
Ecclesiastes 10:1

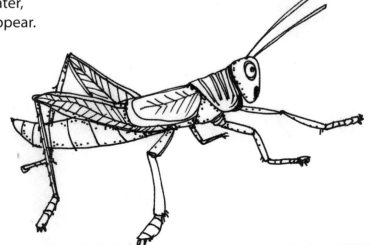

ARMY OF BONES

The hand of the Lord was on Ezekiel,
A prophet whom God greatly cherished,
When God brought him to a valley of bones,
Where a great many men once had perished.

With piles of bones—skulls, ulnas, and ribs—
The entire valley was dotted.
Wherever he looked, Ezekiel saw bones
From bodies that long ago rotted.

God asked His prophet, "Can these bones still live?"
"Only You know" was Ezekiel's word.
So God said to him, "Speak to the dry bones.
Say, 'Bones, hear the word of the Lord!'

"'I'll make you alive, put breath in your lungs,
Give you muscles and tendons and skin.
You will rise back to life, no longer dead bones.'"
Then God said to Ezekiel, "Begin."

Ezekiel repeated each word that God said,
Addressing the valley of bones.
They rattled aloud while they rose up at once
As skeletons that stood on their own.

Next came the muscles and skin and the rest
Till they looked like real human men.
But they still didn't breathe till God told Ezekiel
To call them to taste air right then.

When Ezekiel did that, they all came alive,
An army of men stood again.
God had taken the dead and given new life,
Granting hope to His earthly children.

➲ **Ezekiel 37:1–14**

icky sticky

LEPERS CHANGE THEIR SPOTS

As Jesus traveled near a town,
He heard a distant fuss.
Ten men with leprosy called out,
"Dear Master, please help us!"

These leprous men had a disease
That made them look disgusting.
Their skin was splotchy, sick, and pale,
And many sores were busting.

Leprosy made toes fall off,
And some feared it would spread.
So they had thrown these men from town
As if already dead.

But when Christ Jesus heard them shout,
His heart was filled with love.
He said, "Go show the priest your skin.
Prove what you've been cleaned of."

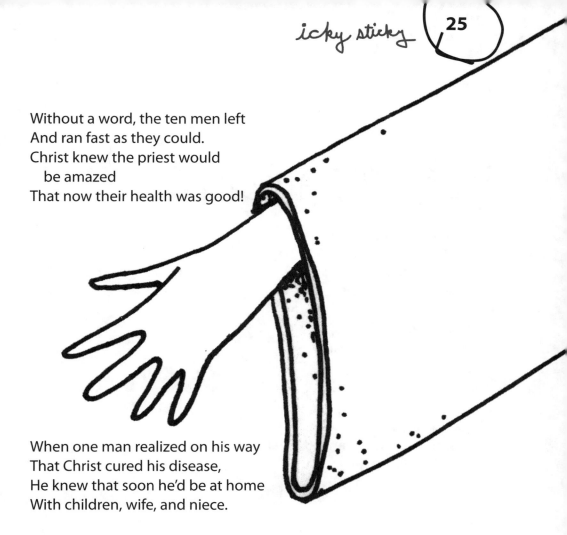

Without a word, the ten men left
And ran fast as they could.
Christ knew the priest would
   be amazed
That now their health was good!

When one man realized on his way
That Christ cured his disease,
He knew that soon he'd be at home
With children, wife, and niece.

Before that, though, he hurried back
To kneel at Jesus' feet.
With teary eyes, he thanked his Lord
For healing so complete.

Then Jesus said, "Where are the nine?
Didn't ten for My help yell?
Yet you alone give praise to God.
Now go—faith made you well."

↪ Luke 17:11–19

HEAD ON A PLATE

You might recall John
And his buggy meals
And how he preached Jesus,
Who rescues and heals.

Well, not too much later,
John was thrown into jail
By a ruler who feared
The truth John would tell.

This king had a party
Where his bad niece danced great,
So he offered a gift—
She chose head on a plate.

That made the king sad,
But he also was weak.
So John's head was cut off—
The death of the meek.

⊃ **Matthew 14:1–12**

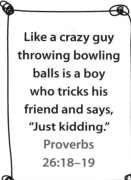

Like a crazy guy throwing bowling balls is a boy who tricks his friend and says, "Just kidding."
Proverbs 26:18–19

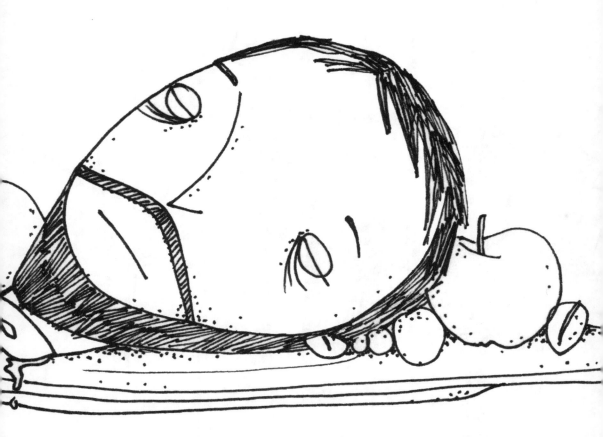

A PIT, A BLOODY COAT, AND PRISON TIME

Joseph had ten older bros
Who thought he was a brat.
Their daddy loved Joseph the most,
Though he tattled like a rat.

Worse, Joe flashed a snazzy coat
Nicer than what they wore
And said he'd dreamt Mom, Dad,
    and they
Himself would bow before.

Those brothers got so mad,
    they tossed
Joe in a filthy pit;
Then took his fancy coat to Dad,
With goat blood staining it.

They told their pop their bro
    was dead—
It broke the old man's heart.
But really they'd sold Joe and said,
"A slave's life you'll now start."

Though Joe became a lowly slave
Away in Egyptland,
God was with him all the way,
And blessed Joe as He'd planned.

Joe worked to be a top-notch slave,
Until a woman lied
And had him thrown into a jail
Where other men had died.

Years passed there while Joe became
The jailer's right-hand guy.
Joe translated prisoners' dreams
Till hope God did supply.

God let Joseph help the king,
Who then gave Joe great power.
And sure enough, Joe's brothers came
To Joe to bow and cower.

➲ **Genesis 37; 39:1–42:6**

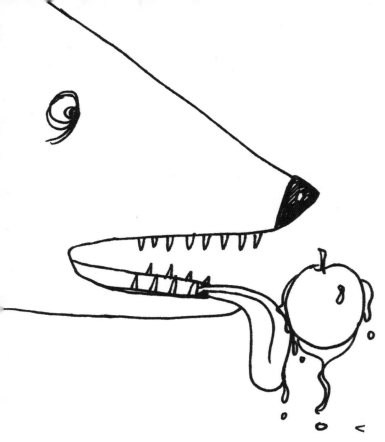

LICKED BY DOGS
AND LICKED BY FLAMES

Lord Jesus told a parable
About a man who had so much
He threw himself a feast each day
Of lamb and cakes and such.

Outside his house, poor Lazarus lay,
His skin covered with oozing sores.
He hungered just to eat a crumb
Or lick old apple cores.

And though the rich man wasted lots
And crumbs fell to the ground,
The only tasting Lazarus got
Came from the tongues of hounds.

Though both men died when
   it was time,
Their final home was not the same.
While Lazarus went to heaven's joy,
The rich man suffered hellish flame.

Worse than a million paper cuts,
The rich man's pain was awful bad,
Especially when far off he saw
That Lazarus was calm and glad.

The rich man yelled to Abraham,
Who stood by Lazarus's side,
"Please send that poor man down to me
With water for my tongue so fried!"

Wise Abraham called back to him,
"Though you were rich in life,
You doubted still our God's true Word,
While Lazarus got pain and strife.

"So now it's only fitting that
You feel the pain you've earned,
While Lazarus gets mercy rich,
Since he for God's help yearned."

➲ **Luke 16:19–25**

icky sticky

TAKE A SANDAL, TAKE A WIFE

Boaz wanted to marry Ruth,
Naomi's daughter, true and kind.
But Boaz had to face the law
Before their hearts could bind.

First, there was another man
Who sought Naomi's land.
To buy it, though, he had to take
In marriage poor Ruth's hand.

"No way," the man said. "That deal stinks.
It might help Ruth, but I get squat.
If you want to marry her,
The land I'll say you've bought."

"And just to show," the man added,
"That Ruth belongs with you,
Here's my sandal proving it,"
And Boaz took his sweaty shoe.

➲ **Ruth 3:9–4:10**

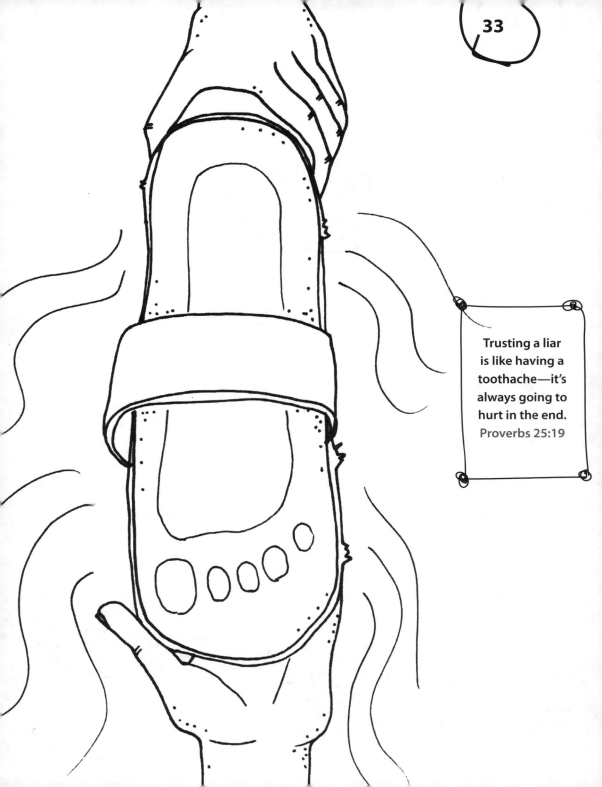

Trusting a liar
is like having a
toothache—it's
always going to
hurt in the end.
Proverbs 25:19

icky sticky

FALLING TO PIECES AND GOLDEN MICE

The ark of the covenant
Was Israel's pride—
A box lined with gold
Where God did abide.

But Israel was foolish,
So God's ark was taken
By Philistine warriors
To the temple of Dagon.

Dagon was a statue,
Their precious false god.
And they set up the ark
Right next to this fraud.

The next morning, though,
"Mighty" Dagon was lying
Face down to God's ark,
A message implying.

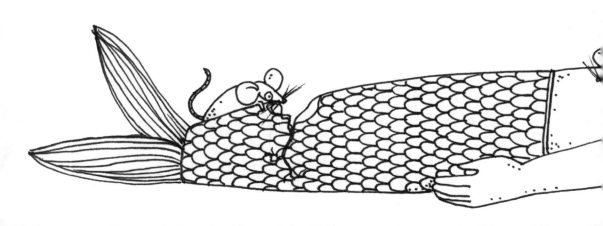

The priests in the temple
Chose this sign to ignore.
They set Dagon back up
And went home to snore.

When they came the next day,
Dagon once more had flopped,
And his head and his hands
From his body were chopped.

Then rats brought a plague
Of tumors and sores.
Throughout their whole land
Rose agonized roars.

Scared, they made tumors
And rats out of gold.
On a wagon they sent
The ark from their stronghold.

⮑ **1 Samuel 4:1–11; 5:1–6:11**

icky sticky

ATTACK OF THE DEMON PIGS!

After Jesus crossed the sea,
He stepped out of His boat
And was met there by a man
Who smelled worse than a goat.

Though people bound this strange guy up,
Each time he broke the chain;
Then hit himself with rocks and shrieked
Amidst the tombs, insane.

Jesus knew immediately
That demons were inside,
And when Christ asked, the demons said,
"Many here abide."

"Come out of him," Lord Jesus said.
"Please, please," the demons begged,
"Let us go into those pigs."
The Lord said, "Go ahead."

The evil spirits left the man
And possessed each piggy.
Two thousand swine ran off the cliff
And drowned there in the sea.

➲ **Mark 5:1–13**

icky sticky

MUCKING AROUND

Jeremiah the prophet spoke clearly God's words
Of death and destruction to come.
But some in the city did not like that news
And plotted to have him undone.

They grabbed Jeremiah and took him away.
They tossed him into a deep hole,
A place where he sank in the mud and the muck,
With escape an impossible goal.

Ebed, the king's man, found out what they'd done
And asked for help from the king.
The king said, "Go get him. Don't let the man die."
So Ebed grabbed rags and a team.

Ebed's team of men ran off to the pit,
Where the prophet was wasting away.
With rope and with rags, they pulled the man out
With a plop from his long muddy stay.

➲ **Jeremiah 38:1–13**

It's better to munch on broccoli with your friends than to have a pizza party with kids who are mean.
Proverbs 15:17

THE PLAGUES:
THE BEGINNING
AND BLOODY WATER

Long, long ago in Egyptland,
God chose a special man
To make His people free again,
To carry out His plan.

This man named Moses whined a lot,
But God just shook His head.
"Take your brother; seek the king;
Tell him what I have said."

Brother Aaron and Moses went
To Pharaoh—that's the king—
And said, "Release the Israelites,
Our people, from slaving."

Then God made Aaron's staff a snake,
And Pharaoh's wizards did the same.
Though Aaron's serpent ate theirs up,
That Pharaoh had no shame.

Proud old Pharaoh laughed
   and mocked,
And he refused to see
That their God was strong enough
To set His people free.

Since Pharaoh was so hard of heart,
God made a plan to send
Ten plagues of horror and of might,
Great Pharaoh's will to bend.

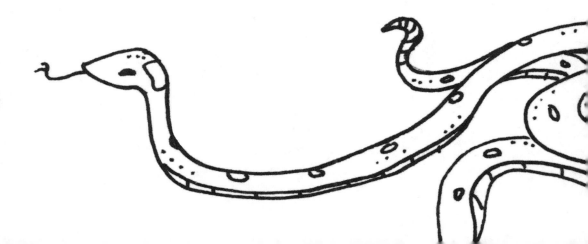

So Moses and his bro once more
Sought Pharaoh and his men
And said, "Now let God's people go!
Behold His power again!"

Plague 1 came forth as Aaron's staff
Stretched o'er the Nile's flood,
And all the river's water deep
Turned into thick red blood.

➲ **Exodus 3:7–4:17; 7**

THE PLAGUES: FROGS, GNATS, FLIES, DEAD ANIMALS, AND BOILS

For seven days after the blood,
Mean Pharaoh did refuse
To set the enslaved Israelites free,
So God brought more plague news.

Plague 2 was frogs, a sea of green
That hopped out from the Nile.
In houses, ovens, and on beds
It seemed they'd stay awhile.

This ribbeting drove Pharaoh mad,
And he begged for an end,
Making pretty promises
That he would later bend.

Still, Moses said, "Okay, we'll see."
And God killed those frogs off.
But Pharaoh said, "I didn't mean it.
That was just a cough."

God struck back fast with number 3,
A million billion gnats
That covered every man and beast,
The dogs and goats and cats.

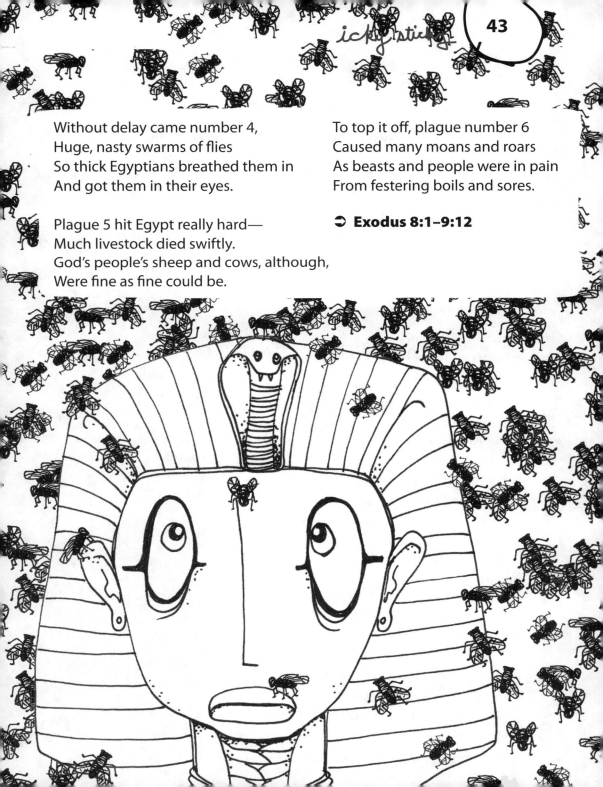

icky sticky

Without delay came number 4,
Huge, nasty swarms of flies
So thick Egyptians breathed them in
And got them in their eyes.

Plague 5 hit Egypt really hard—
Much livestock died swiftly.
God's people's sheep and cows, although,
Were fine as fine could be.

To top it off, plague number 6
Caused many moans and roars
As beasts and people were in pain
From festering boils and sores.

➲ **Exodus 8:1–9:12**

THE PLAGUES: HAIL, LOCUSTS, DARKNESS, AND DEATH

Some folks might think with all the pain
The plagues had brought his way,
Pharaoh would give up at last,
Send Israel away.

But his heart was hard as stone,
So God had more in store.
Plague 7's hail killed off the crops,
The animals, and more.

Fire and thunder too arose,
While hail bashed left and right.
Pharaoh said to Moses, "Stop!
You all may leave my sight."

Moses prayed, and that hail stopped,
But Pharaoh broke his word.
So next, plague 8 swarmed in the land:
A countless locust horde!

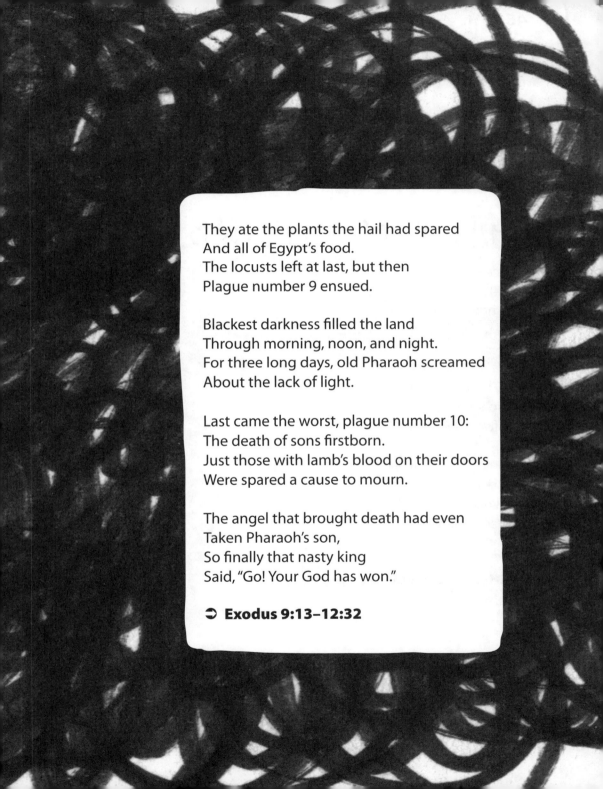

They ate the plants the hail had spared
And all of Egypt's food.
The locusts left at last, but then
Plague number 9 ensued.

Blackest darkness filled the land
Through morning, noon, and night.
For three long days, old Pharaoh screamed
About the lack of light.

Last came the worst, plague number 10:
The death of sons firstborn.
Just those with lamb's blood on their doors
Were spared a cause to mourn.

The angel that brought death had even
Taken Pharaoh's son,
So finally that nasty king
Said, "Go! Your God has won."

➲ **Exodus 9:13–12:32**

icky sticky

WHAT'S FOR DINNER?

God once gave a list
For Israel's diet
Of stuff not to eat,
Though they bake, boil, or fry it:

No camels, no lizards,
No pigs, hawks, or eels,
No ostriches, butterflies,
Or bats for their meals.

They could chew, however,
On cabbage and cricket,
With gazelle garlic soup—
Such a tasty meal ticket.

⊃ Leviticus 11; Deuteronomy 14:1–21

Too much junk food makes you sick, and bragging about how great you are makes other people sick of you.
Proverbs 25:27

icky sticky

FOOT HAIR
AND A GREAT SINNER

"It's dinnertime, Jesus,"
Said the Pharisee.
"So hurry up now
And come eat with me."

Jesus went to his house
And sat with the guests—
Fancy folks all,
The best of the best.

A woman came in then,
A terrible sinner,
Though never invited
To the Pharisee's dinner.

She wept beside Jesus.
Her tears fell right there,
Dropping onto His feet,
Which she wiped with her hair.

Then she kissed Christ's dear feet
And rubbed ointment in,
Showing care for His toenails
And ankles and skin.

But the Pharisee thought,
"If this Jesus were great,
He'd have called her a sinner,
Sent her away straight."

Jesus knew what he thought
And said, "You're a poor host.
You gave Me no washing
Or welcome or toast.

"This woman, though, gave with
Each tear, hair, and touch,
For great sinners forgiven
Tend to love very much."

➲ **Luke 7:36–50**

icky sticky

GETTING CLEAN IN DIRTY WATER

Long before Christ Jesus healed
Ten men with leprosy,
An army chief named Naaman
Had this same skin disease.

There was no hope for Naaman
Until a girl, a slave,
Who once had lived in Israel
Advice to his wife gave.

She said, "One prophet near my home
Can heal most anything."
So Naaman's boss sent him to get
Some help from Israel's king.

Israel's king tore his own clothes.
"I am not God!" he cried.
But the prophet sent a note:
"Have him come to my side."

When Naaman's horse-drawn chariots
Sped to the prophet's place,
A messenger instead came out
To speak the prophet's case:

"Prophet Elisha says to wash
Seven times in Jordan's stream.
And then your illness God will heal."
Naaman, though, began to scream.

"The Jordan's mucky," Naaman whined.
His servants said, "Just go."
So he washed there seven times,
And God healed all his woe.

Though the healed man offered gifts,
Elisha shook his head.
But when a greedy helper stole,
He got leprosy instead.

➲ **2 Kings 5**

icky sticky

THE ROTTEN BUZZ

Some people get their food from stores
Or gardens filled with munchies.
But Samson found a different way
To make one of his lunches.

Near some vines of juicy grapes,
An angry lion saw him,
Roared at him, and bared sharp teeth—
It was about to maul him.

Samson, though, didn't like that plan,
So instead he killed the lion.
He tore it fiercely limb from limb
Until the beast was dyin'.

He left the body in the dust
And went about his business.
Yet later on when he walked past,
From the lion he heard buzzes.

"Man, that's odd," strong Samson thought,
"I was sure that I had killed it."
When he looked close, it was still dead,
But something else had filled it.

What was in the lion's corpse
Was really, oh, so funny.
Samson laughed at this strange sight:
Lion filled with bees and honey.

Then Samson's stomach gave a growl,
And honey he took for eating.
Out of a beast so dead and foul,
God gave to him a sweet thing.

➲ **Judges 14:5–11**

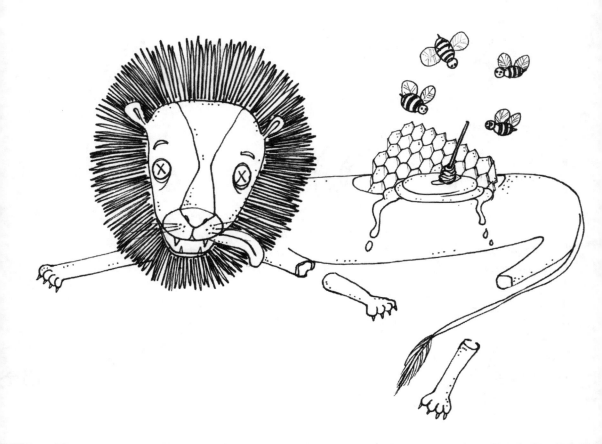

icky sticky

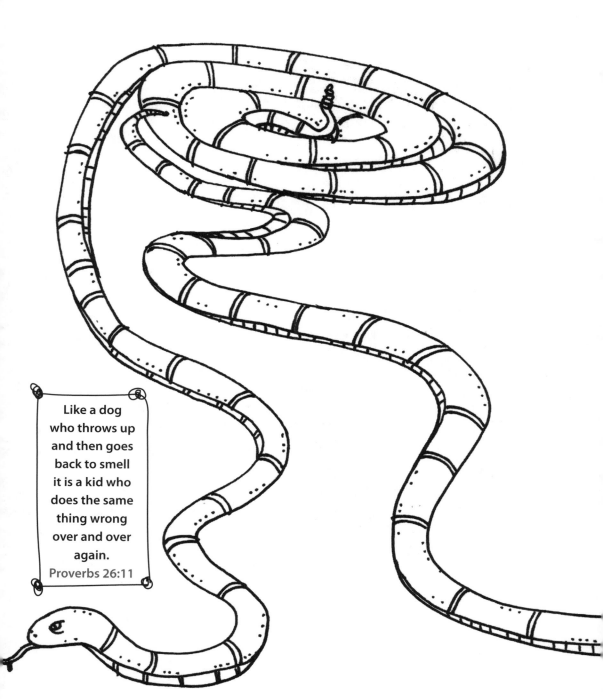

Like a dog who throws up and then goes back to smell it is a kid who does the same thing wrong over and over again.
Proverbs 26:11

SNAKES AND SCORPIONS

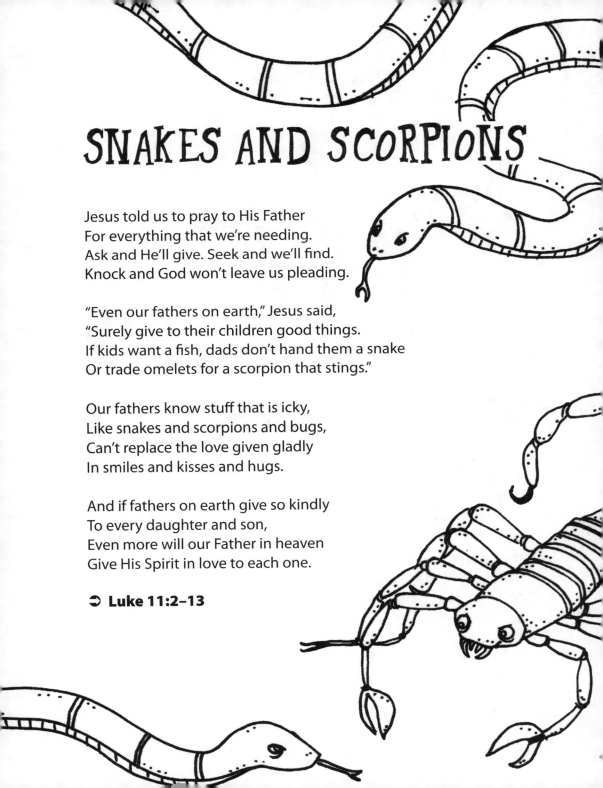

Jesus told us to pray to His Father
For everything that we're needing.
Ask and He'll give. Seek and we'll find.
Knock and God won't leave us pleading.

"Even our fathers on earth," Jesus said,
"Surely give to their children good things.
If kids want a fish, dads don't hand them a snake
Or trade omelets for a scorpion that stings."

Our fathers know stuff that is icky,
Like snakes and scorpions and bugs,
Can't replace the love given gladly
In smiles and kisses and hugs.

And if fathers on earth give so kindly
To every daughter and son,
Even more will our Father in heaven
Give His Spirit in love to each one.

⟳ **Luke 11:2–13**

SWINE AND DINE

Once a good man and his two sons
Lived in true harmony,
Until one day the youngest said,
"Gimme! Gimme! Gimme!"

And though the son had asked for things
He should not yet have had,
He and his brother both received
Great gifts from their kind dad.

The younger son soon ran away
With his vast newfound wealth,
Ignoring all his father's love
And thinking of himself.

With these fine treasures he now had,
The friends he found were many—
Getting fat and getting drunk
And spending every penny.

He and his friends did sinful things
While he spent his whole stash.
And then these non-friends
   left him too—
No hope, no food, no cash.

The son next took the awful job
Of feeding pods to swine.
His belly hungered so badly
That slop looked mighty fine.

Feeling like he would soon die,
To home he aimed to run
To beg his dad to let him be
A servant, not a son.

The father, though, saw him approach,
Ran to him, hugged, and cried.
He said, "My son is home! Let's feast!
He'll never leave my side."

⮑ **Luke 15:11–24**

ALL TORN UP

Queen Jezebel was as mean as they got,
Evil as evil could be.
She worshiped fake gods and had prophets killed.
"Death be to them all!" cried she.

Queen Jez was so bad she once killed a man
Just to get his garden of grapes.
So when the news came that justice was planned,
You'd think she'd try to escape.

But this queen instead put on makeup and frills,
Dressing fancy as soldiers came near.
Showing no shame, she glared down from her room,
Screamed, "Traitors!" and gave them a sneer.

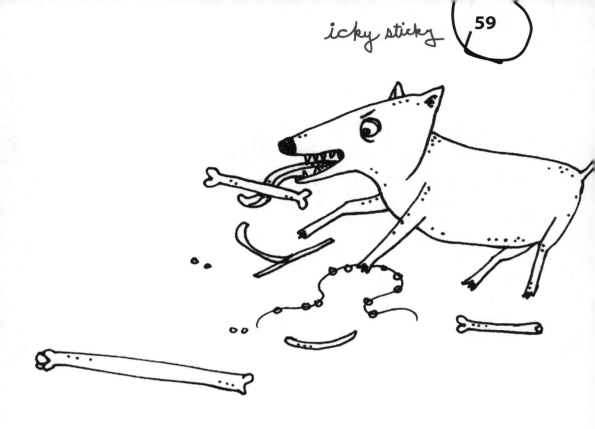

Then Jehu, the king of the men on the ground,
Shouted out to the servants upstairs,
"Who's with me?" And two or three threw Jezebel
Out the window and into midair.

Well, that was the end of Jezebel's life
Since it was a long fall to the street.
She crashed to the ground in a big bloody mess,
And Jehu went inside to eat.

After they dined, Jehu sent out his men
To bury that evilest of all.
But the dogs had eaten and torn her apart,
Leaving only her hands, feet, and skull.

➲ **1 Kings 18:13; 21:1–16; 2 Kings 9:30–37**

FOUR DAYS DEAD

A man named Lazarus was so sick
His sisters called Jesus for aid.
But it took Jesus several more days
Till at last a visit He made.

When He arrived, Jesus was told
That Lazarus was four days dead!
And Lazarus's sisters said to Jesus,
"If You'd been here, he'd live instead."

Sad for His friend, Lord Jesus wept
Outside where Lazarus was buried.
But when Christ wanted the tomb opened up,
Some feared the stench the grave carried.

Still they moved the stone, and Jesus announced,
"Lazarus, come out now from death!"
Then mummylike Lazarus stepped out alive
And praised God with his every breath!

➲ John 11:1–44

> **It is better to be stuck
> alone in the middle of
> the desert than
> to be at home with
> a girl who picks fights
> all the time.**
> Proverbs 21:19

icky sticky

WEIRD MUSHY STUFF

Of all the weird and icky stuff
The Bible has inside,
Nothing tops the Song of Songs,
Its mushy groom and bride.

First the man, who's really odd,
Says, "She is like a horse,
Pulling a cart into a war,
But wearing jewels, of course."

Then she says, "He's like a tree
That's growing in the woods.
Because I love him, oh, so much,
I'm sick, but that is good."

So he says, "She's a lily
That grows near thorns prickling."
And she says, "My dear man's voice
Is sweet when it's yelling."

She goes on, "He leaps o'er hills
Like a gazelle or stag.
And now foxes are stealing grapes,
But he'll catch them in a bag."

Barely blushing, he says next,
"Her birdlike eyes are deep.
Her hair is like a bunch of goats.
Her teeth are like bald sheep.

"Her cheeks are fruit," he whispers sweet.
"Her neck is like a tower.
Run away from leopards now,
And from the lions cower."

Then both stare all lovey-dovey
And give a lot of kisses.
"Kissy. Kissy. Kissy. Kissy,"
Say both mister and missus.

⮌ Song of Solomon

NEVER TOO ICKY OR STICKY FOR GOD

So whether you eat bugs or slop
Or honey from a corpse
Or swallow cows or scorpions
Or you're a worm's main course

And whether you are stuck in muck
Or you're inside a fish—
Even if your head's cut off
And sitting on a dish—

Remember that God loves you still,
And His Son came to save,
To wash your sin—not just your feet—
To raise you from the grave.

And spit and bones and splotchy skin,
Demon pigs and rotten friends,
And dogs and kissy lips and plagues
Won't keep you from the love God sends.

➲ **Romans 8:31–39**

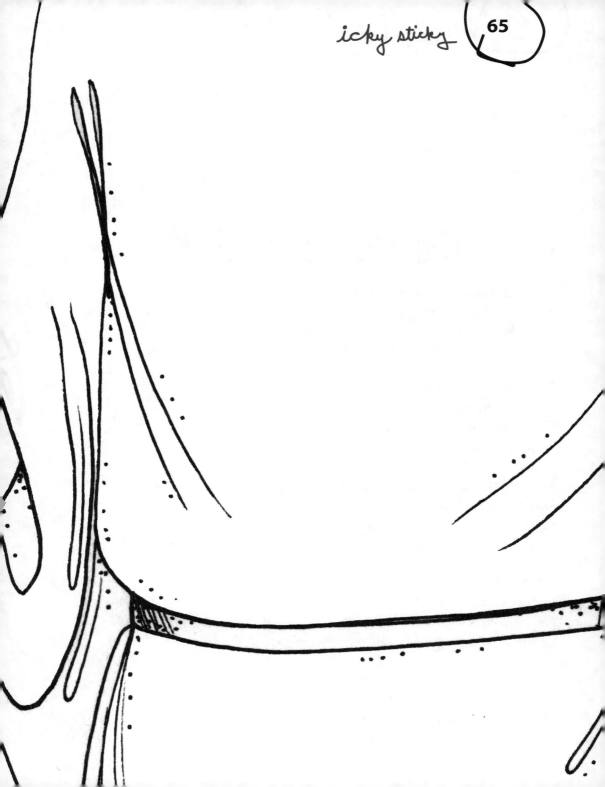

A BATHRoOM BREAK?

Bad King Ahab worshiped Baal
And lots of other fake gods too.
He tricked the people with Baal's priests,
A four-hundred-fifty-prophet crew.

God's man Elijah hated this,
So he offered up a test:
"Send your prophets to the mount.
We'll prove then which god is best."

At the mountain these men gathered,
And all the people came to see.
Elijah said, "Give us two bulls—
One for them and one for me.

"I'll take turns with Baal's guys there
To pray to heaven and exclaim.
We'll see which god is truly God
By which one burns the bull with flame."

So Baal's four hundred fifty men
Took their bull and danced around.
They prayed, shouted, and cut themselves,
But from their god they heard no sound.

"Answer us, O Baal!" they cried
Until the morning turned to noon.
Elijah mocked, "Is he asleep
Or maybe stuck in his bathroom?"

Elijah put his bull on wood
And dug around it a deep trench.
On the bull he had them pour
Enough water to fully drench.

Elijah prayed, "God, answer me!"
And water, wood, and bull were flamed!
The people shouted, "God is Lord."
By death Baal's prophets then were claimed.

⊃ **1 Kings 18:17–40**

hairy scary

BRIMSTONE WITH A TOUCH OF SALT

There once were two cities,
Gomorrah and Sodom,
That were totally wicked
From the top to the bottom.

God planned to destroy them
And wipe out this sin,
But Abraham begged Him
To spare Lot, his kin.

Lot, Abraham's nephew,
Dwelt in Sodom town,
So God sent two angels
To get the lowdown.

Looking like humans,
To Sodom they went.
Then Lot took them home,
Not asking a cent.

When the townsfolk heard
Of the visitors there,
These people so nasty
Ran straight through the square.

They knocked on Lot's door
And made evil requests.
Lot said dumb stuff too
But protected his guests.

Lot's guests told his family,
"Don't look back!" and "Run!"
For brimstone would fall
Soon after dawn's sun.

Though all of Lot's family
Escaped the assault,
His wife glanced behind her
And was turned into salt.

➲ **Genesis 18:20–19:29**

CHICKENS OF THE SEA

Christ Jesus said one evening,
"Let's go across the lake."
So He and His disciples twelve
Chose their boat to take.

While Jesus snoozed beneath the stern,
The boat began to shake.
The waves grew large; the wind roared past.
Afraid, the Twelve did quake.

The water filled the boat till they
Thought it would sink right down.
Terrified, they woke up Christ:
"Do You want us to drown?"

Jesus called to wind and sea,
"Peace! Be still, I say!"
And just like that, the water calmed.
The storm had gone away.

"Have you no faith?" He asked the Twelve.
"You guys are so not brave."
They asked themselves, "Who is this man
Who commands wind and wave?"

➲ **Mark 4:35–41**

hairy scary

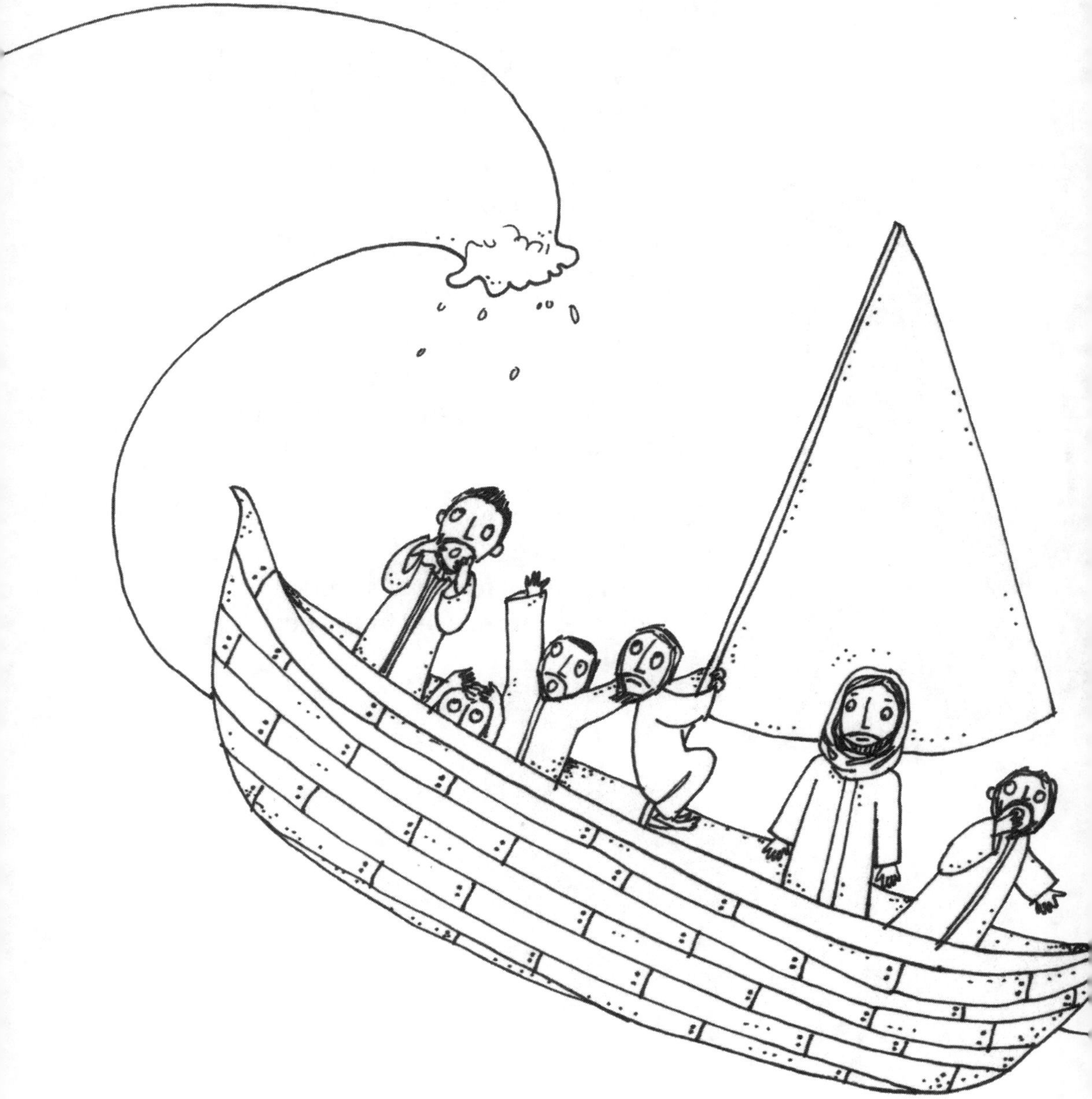

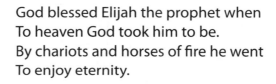

BALDY, THE BOYS, AND THE BEARS

God blessed Elijah the prophet when
To heaven God took him to be.
By chariots and horses of fire he went
To enjoy eternity.

This made things tough for Elisha though,
Whom God gave Elijah's old job.
He got no respect, and the people doubted
Elijah had gone up to God.

The worst was a group of boys who yelled,
"Hey, baldy! You go up too!"
Elisha cursed them for being so rude,
And two she-bears mauled forty-two.

⮷ **2 Kings 2:11–25**

Like a water
fountain that
shoots mud is
a good kid who
does stuff he
knows is wrong.
Proverbs 25:26

LIONS AND TIGERS AND SKUNKS—PHEW!

"The world is so evil,"
God sadly declared.
"I'll wipe them all out."
Still, for Noah He cared.

So God said to Noah,
"Build yourself a boat,
A massive wood ark,
And to safety you'll float.

"Bring animal pairs,
Your sons, and their wives.
I'll spare you, Mrs. Noah,
And your family's lives."

Noah got to it,
Constructing his ship.
But the people nearby
Said, "Man, get a grip."

When Noah had finished,
The zoo came to town,
As animals showed up
So they wouldn't drown.

With cobras and hippos,
With bears, skunks, and lynx
Crammed in that one boat—
Imagine the stinks!

For forty days rain
Destroyed all the rest,
But Noah and fam'ly
Were saved and were blest.

They landed and praised God.
And God promised them
By a rainbow to not flood
The whole world again.

➲ Genesis 6:5–9:17

hairy scary

·DEAD SLEEP

The people knew that Christ was strong,
That He was good and wise.
He'd healed the sick and paralyzed
And wiped tears from their eyes.

But when a man named Jairus said,
"My daughter's deadly ill,"
Many likely wondered whether
Jesus her could heal.

Her daddy said, "Please, Jesus, come.
Touch her, and she will live."
So Jesus followed to the house
With gifts of God to give.

People ran out from the house
To say, "The girl has died.
Don't bug Jesus anymore.
He need not come inside."

Jesus said to Jairus then,
"Don't fear. Faith you must keep."
And to the folks who wept and wailed,
"Hush up. She's just asleep."

Though the people laughed at Him,
Christ Jesus walked inside.
With three disciples, Mom, and Dad,
He went to her bedside.

Though she was dead—make no mistake—
Kind Jesus took her hand.
"Arise, sweet little girl," He said.
Then she rose up to stand.

The girl began to walk around.
Her parents' joy did swell!
Jesus said, "Give this girl grub,
And what I've done don't tell."

➲ **Luke 8:40–42, 49–56**

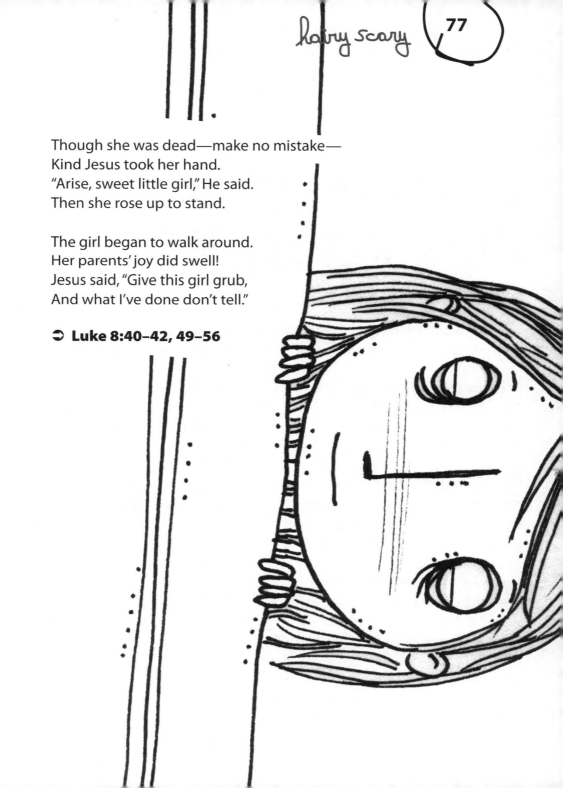

A WATERY SAVE AND A WATERY GRAVE

When Pharaoh at last let Moses take
The Israelites from Egyptland,
God led them to the Red Sea's shore
With pillars of smoke and fire grand.

Pharaoh, though, had changed his mind
And rushed his army after them.
With horses, chariots, and spears,
These people he sought to condemn.

Israel's people cried in fear,
"Did God bring us out to our doom?
We could have stayed as Egypt's slaves,
But now this desert is our tomb!"

Moses said, "Fear not! Stand firm!
The Lord, our God, will fight for you.
He will defeat the pharaoh's troops.
Quit yapping! Watch what God will do!"

Then God told Moses, "Raise your staff,
And stretch your hand out toward the sea."
When Moses did as God had asked,
The large waves split in two neatly.

Between those two huge water walls,
God made a path of land well dried
For Israel's people forth to go
And walk through to the other side.

Many thousands walked that path,
While God sent out a massive cloud
To block proud Egypt's army men
From getting near to Israel's crowd.

At last when Israel was through
And Pharaoh's army followed close,
God made the Red Sea walls crash
   down—
His people safe, but death to foes.

⊃ **Exodus 13:17–14:31**

A CLIFF HANGER

After Jesus had journeyed
And taught many places,
He traveled back home
To see kindly faces.

On the Sabbath He preached
That God truly sent Him
To give the blind sight,
To give hope to the grim.

They said, "But we know You,
So that can't be true."
He said, "Can a prophet
Not pass your review?"

The crowd there went crazy
And tried that same day
To throw Christ off a cliff,
But He just walked away.

➲ **Luke 4:14–30**

A son who makes dumb choices makes his dad miserable, and a girl who argues all the time is like a loud leaky faucet.

Proverbs 19:13

LION BREATH

King Darius's right-hand man,
Daniel, rocked at everything.
This made the politicians mad
As to power they tried to cling.

Knowing Daniel loved the Lord,
They tricked the king to make a law
That praying unto God would be
A deadly and illegal flaw.

This didn't stop Dan's faithful prayers,
So these tricksters turned him in.
The king was angry and quite sad
To toss Dan in the lions' den.

The king called down to Daniel there,
"I hope your God protects you now."
But when a stone sealed Daniel in,
It looked like he was lion chow.

The lions' teeth were sharp and white.
Their bellies rumbled to be filled.
Their breath smelled like raw sewage pits.
Surely Daniel would be killed!

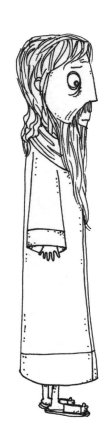

hairy scary

King Darius stayed up all night;
He didn't eat and didn't sleep.
Then when the sun rose, he ran off
To see if Dan was lion meat.

The king asked, "Daniel, are you there?
Did the lions rip you up?"
Daniel shouted, "God is good!
His angel kept the beasts' mouths shut."

Daniel came out of the den,
And Darius without a pause
Threw those tricky men inside
To meet the lions' hungry jaws.

➲ **Daniel 6**

A HAIRY SCARY MAN

The sons of Rebekah
And Isaac were twins
Who looked nothing alike,
Even down to their skins.

While Esau, the older,
Was hairy and strong,
Jacob was smooth
And as gentle as song.

Though God had decided
To bless Jacob more,
Rebekah and Isaac
Turned this into war.

Isaac chose Esau
To lead their clan's crew,
But Esau sold Jacob
This right for some stew.

As Isaac grew older
And could see much less,
He said to big Esau,
"Son, you I will bless.

"Go hunt down some food;
Then I will bless you."
Rebekah heard, though,
And had a plan too.

She gave Jacob food,
On his skin put goat hair,
And Isaac was tricked
The best blessing to share.

Though Esau was murderous
And Jacob left home,
After years of this exile,
Peace later would come.

⊃ **Genesis 25:21–34;
27:1–45**

SNAKE ON A STICK

God freed Israel from Egypt,
Saved them through the sea,
Gave them manna and water,
Trounced Pharaoh's army.

Yet still they complained
Against Moses and God,
"Did you bring us all out here
To our deaths to trod?

"There's no food or water,"
They out-and-out lied.
"Plus we're tired of manna,
And it's worthless besides."

Sick of their whining,
God sent snakes of fire
That bit many people,
Causing lives to expire.

Shaking with pain
And fearful of death,
The people told Moses,
"We've sinned with each breath.

"We're sorry for griping
At God and at you.
Please beg Him to save us
From this serpent crew."

So Moses said prayers,
And God told him to
Make a serpent of bronze
For the bitten to view.

Then all those snakebitten
Who'd been deathly sick
Were healed by their Lord
And His snake on a stick.

➲ **Numbers 21:4–9**

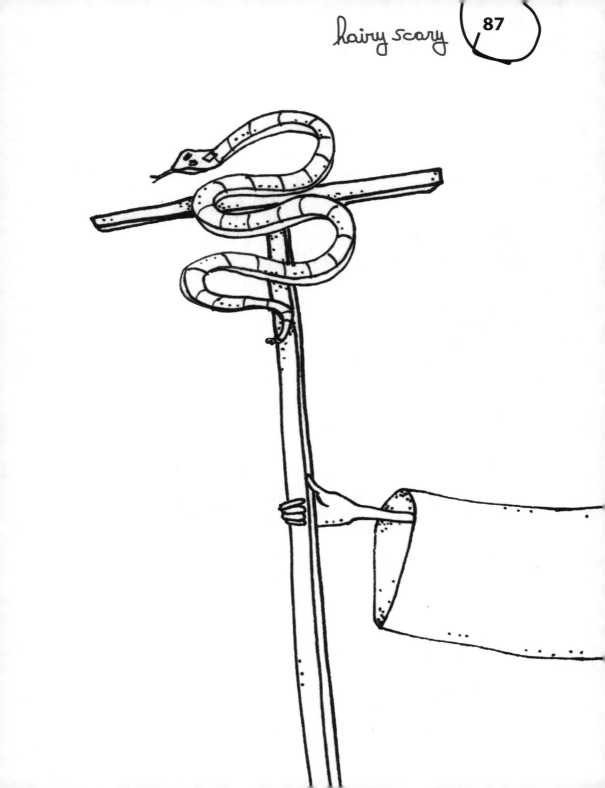

ALMOST ROADKILL

The Lord told a story:
"A man once was beaten,
Robbed, and then left
For the vultures to eat him.

"Along came a priest
And a church worker too,
Yet both men ignored him
And walked out of view.

"But one that he hated,
A Samaritan man,
Bound up his wounds
And his healing began.

"The kind man gave money
To show this man care."
Jesus said then,
"Do the same, if you dare."

➲ **Luke 10:25–37**

> **The one who makes fun of his father and disrespects his mother will have his eye plucked out by ravens and gobbled up by vultures.**
> Proverbs 30:17

THE DONKEY AND THE CURSING MAN

In Moses' time of leading God's people,
Enemies many Israel had.
One of these men, King Balak of Moab,
Came up with a plan to do something bad.

He summoned Balaam, whose words had much power,
And begged him to curse each Israelite.
"I only say what God tells me," said Balaam.
"But maybe this time He'll say it's all right."

God said, "Stay put now, and don't curse My people."
Balaam, though, waffled when they offered gold.
Finally, Balaam set off on his donkey,
Thinking that curses could be bought and sold.

God steamed with anger and sent down His angel
With a sword in his hand to block Balaam's way.
Though Balaam saw nothing, the donkey knew better
And turned from the path to wander away.

Three times the donkey avoided the angel,
And three times mad Balaam gave it a smack.
Then God let the donkey speak like a person:
"Tell me what I've done to earn this attack."

"You've made me a fool!" yelled Balaam with fury.
"If I had a sword I'd slice you right now!"
God opened his eyes so he saw the angel,
And Balaam fell with his face to the ground.

The sword-wielding angel said, "You got so lucky.
Your donkey just saved you three times from my sword."
"I'm sorry," said Balaam, "for acts that were evil.
If I should turn back, just please say the word."

The angel said, "Go, but speak only blessings."
So Balaam went down, and that's what he said.
Then Balak was angry and demanded curses,
But only good gifts on God's people were spread.

➲ **Numbers 22–24**

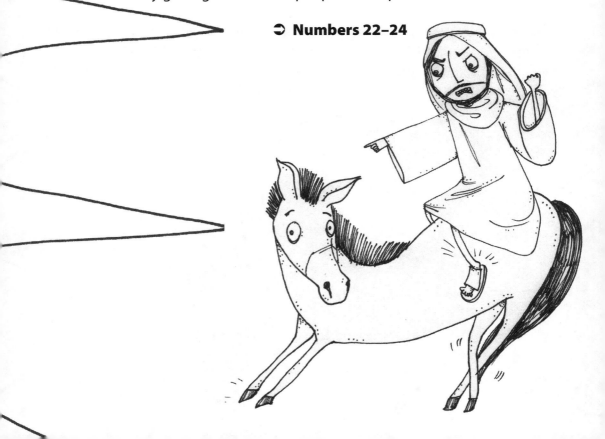

ANGEL SMACKDOWN

Hezekiah was in trouble.
His army was in ruins.
The mighty Assyrian king
Was coming with his goons.

Hezekiah ruled as king
Within Jerusalem,
Which a giant group of troops
Was set to overrun.

Sennacherib, the foreign king,
A messenger sent out
To insult their God and Lord,
To make the people doubt.

The messenger said, "You are doomed
To eat filth and to die!
Just like the gods of other lands,
Your God won't hear your cry!"

When Hezekiah heard these words,
He tore his clothes, then wore a sack.
He went into the temple-church
And begged God to stop this attack.

God heard his prayer and blessed his faith
And sent a prophet to announce,
"Because these foreign guys mock Me,
I surely will their army trounce."

That night, the angel of the Lord
Went to the foreign army den.
He struck down dead as they all slept
One hundred eighty-five thousand men!

➲ **2 Kings 18:17–19:35**

hairy scary

THE KING GETS A HAND

King Belshazzar's great party rocked,
With a thousand of his lords
Drinking wine and acting crude
And saying foolish words.

Immediately, a human hand
Appeared before them all
And carved a secret message there
Into the palace wall.

The king turned white; he nearly fell.
They all were terrified.
Worst of all, the message left
The wisest men tongue-tied.

Then Daniel told them what it meant.
"King, you are full of pride.
Your kingdom and your life are done."
The king that same night died.

➲ **Daniel 5**

מנא
מנא
אתקל
ופרסי
ן

A peaceful heart makes
your body strong, but
always wanting what
others have rots your
bones away.
Proverbs 14:30

hairy scary

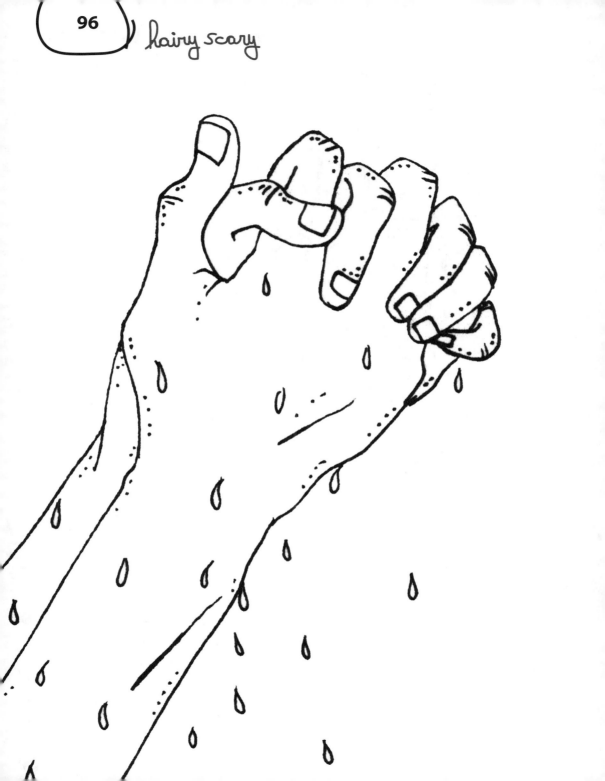

BLOODy SWEAT AND BETRAYAL

Christ led His disciples
To a garden one night.
He told them, "Pray dearly.
Temptation now fight."

Then He went on farther
A short ways away,
Got down on His knees,
And started to pray.

"Dear Father, I ask You,
This cup take from Me.
But Your will, not Mine,
Is what's meant to be."

When He looked, His friends had
All drowsed into sleep.
He scolded, "Be stronger
As your watch you keep."

He prayed yet again,
"Father, if this must be,
Then Your will be done."
And He went back to see.

The disciples, exhausted,
Were snoozing again.
So He left them and prayed
More to God in heaven.

An angel brought strength,
But Christ's sweat was like blood
As He prayed that His Father
Would work all for good.

He woke up His friends
When Judas came near
With a well-weaponed mob
That arrested Christ there.

➲ **Matthew 26:36–50**

THE TRIALS, THE WHIP, AND THE CROSS

From Pilate to Herod
To Pilate again,
Lord Jesus was questioned
By such petty men.

Blindfolded by soldiers
Who beat him and said,
"Now tell us who struck You,"
He silently bled.

Though Pilate tried faintly
To let Jesus go,
The crowd urged, "Crucify!
Let blood on us flow!"

"See here, I have whipped Him,"
Weak Pilate said then.
The nasty whip lashes
Had torn up Christ's skin.

"Kill Him," they repeated,
And Pilate gave in.
So with thorns on His head,
Jesus bore all our sin.

To a hill they led Him.
They nailed hands and feet.
It seemed like the Savior
Had met His defeat.

He cried out, "My God,
Why have You left Me?"
Then He said, "It's finished,"
And He died on the tree.

⊃ **Matthew 27:1–50;**
   Luke 23;
   John 18:28–19:30

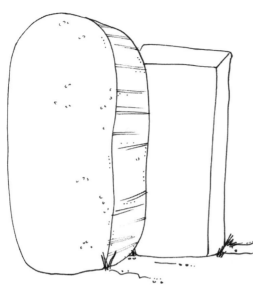

The scariest days ever
Came after that end
For Jesus' disciples,
Each sad, lonely friend.

Their hopes were so high
Till His death on the cross.
Doom and despair
Seemed the price of that loss.

On the third day of crying,
Women went to the tomb
To care for Christ's body
And face their own gloom.

TERRIBLE DAYS AND A BEAUTIFUL MORNING

But angels they found there
In the tomb open wide.
"Fear not," said the angels.
"He has risen who died!"

The glad women hurried
To tell all the boys,
But the menfolk said, "Nah,
This is one of those ploys.

"Perhaps someone's stolen
His body away."
Yet proof Christ had risen
Built up through the day.

Quite late that same evening,
When disciples were hidden,
Jesus came before them,
And with fear they were ridden.

"I'm no ghost," said Jesus,
"I really am here.
Peace be with you now
As you forgive without fear."

➲ **Luke 23:55–24:49;
John 20:19–23**

BULLYING, BLINDNESS, AND A BASKET OF HOPE

Attacking God's Church, Saul dragged people to jail
And threatened disciples of Christ.
But something that happened to him on the road
Changed his life and what he sacrificed.

A bright blazing light tore straight down from heaven,
And a voice said, "Saul, fix your ways.
I'm Jesus, whose people you've persecuted."
And behold! Jesus blinded Saul's gaze.

Blind Saul was led on to a town, where a man
Came to him and brought back his sight.
This man said, "Saul, Jesus calls you His own.
For Him you will be a bright light."

Soon Saul, known as Paul, preached in that same town,
Shocking most and scaring the rest.
Threatened with murder, in a basket he fled.
Then for years, Jesus' love he confessed!

⮑ **Acts 9:1–25**

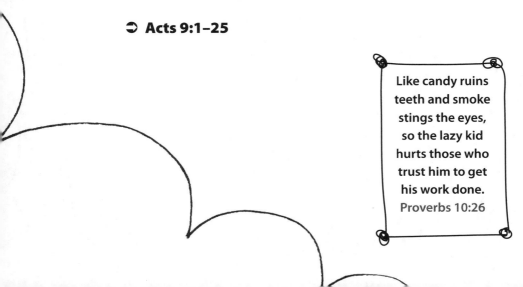

**Like candy ruins
teeth and smoke
stings the eyes,
so the lazy kid
hurts those who
trust him to get
his work done.**
Proverbs 10:26

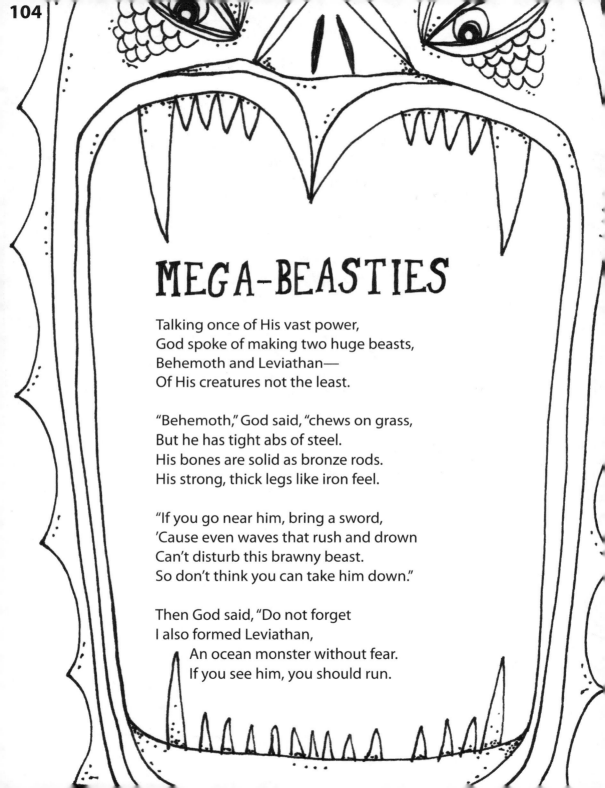

MEGA-BEASTIES

Talking once of His vast power,
God spoke of making two huge beasts,
Behemoth and Leviathan—
Of His creatures not the least.

"Behemoth," God said, "chews on grass,
But he has tight abs of steel.
His bones are solid as bronze rods.
His strong, thick legs like iron feel.

"If you go near him, bring a sword,
'Cause even waves that rush and drown
Can't disturb this brawny beast.
So don't think you can take him down."

Then God said, "Do not forget
I also formed Leviathan,
An ocean monster without fear.
If you see him, you should run.

"Circling his teeth is terror fierce.
His back is made of rows of shields.
His sneezes flash the depths with light,
And smoke and fire his breathing yields.

"His hide is thick. His heart is stone.
Sharp sword and arrow, club and spear
Are puny weapons just like straw
When Leviathan draws near.

"There is not like him any beast.
He makes the deepest oceans churn
And causes manly warriors to
Beg and for their mommies yearn."

➲ **Job 40:15–41:34**

hairy scary

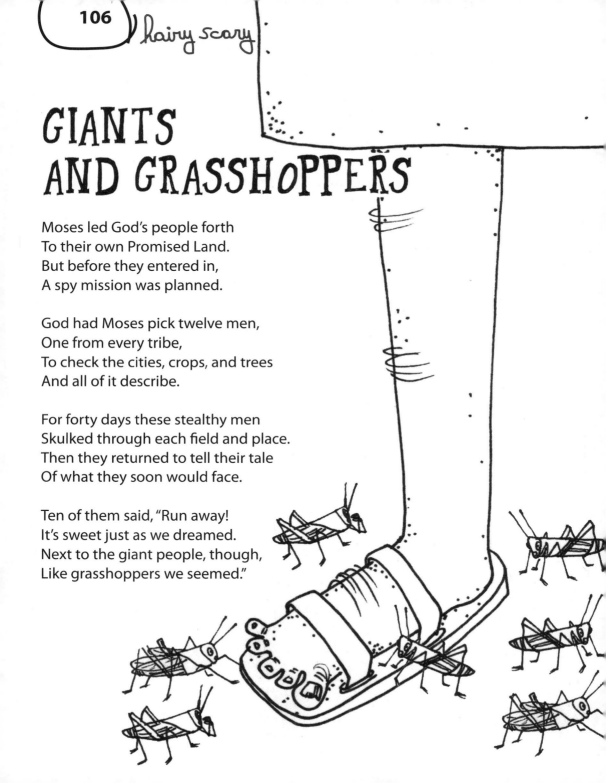

GIANTS AND GRASSHOPPERS

Moses led God's people forth
To their own Promised Land.
But before they entered in,
A spy mission was planned.

God had Moses pick twelve men,
One from every tribe,
To check the cities, crops, and trees
And all of it describe.

For forty days these stealthy men
Skulked through each field and place.
Then they returned to tell their tale
Of what they soon would face.

Ten of them said, "Run away!
It's sweet just as we dreamed.
Next to the giant people, though,
Like grasshoppers we seemed."

The other two, Caleb and Josh,
Said, "Milk and honey flow.
God will give to us this land.
Just trust Him, and let's go!"

The people did what they did best:
They grumbled against God.
They said, "God brought us here to die.
Let's back to Egypt plod."

Then Moses they were going to kill,
So God's voice with rage shook.
For doubting Him they'd have to wait—
Forty long years it took.

➲ **Numbers 13:1–14:38**

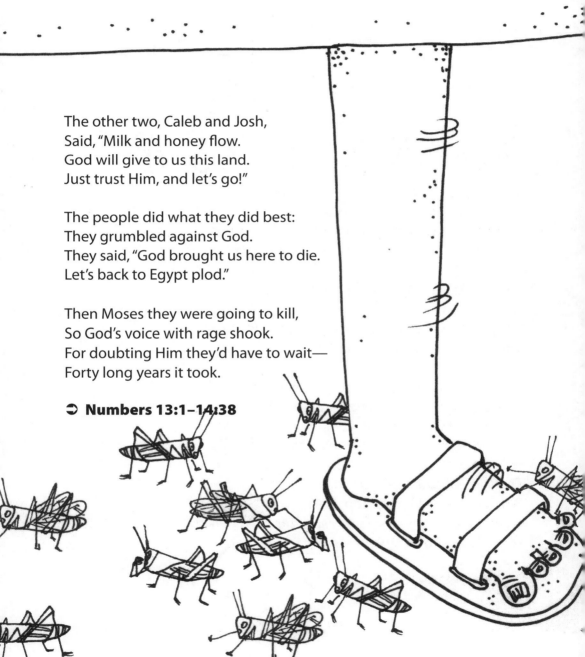

SHAKING THINGS UP

The traveling preachers Silas and Paul
A teller of fortunes had stopped,
So those who'd made money off of the scheme
Said, "These meddling bums should be dropped."

The whole town attacked poor Silas and Paul,
And even the rulers joined in.
They ordered them stripped and beat with a rod.
They hit them again and again.

Paul and Silas were jailed; their feet were locked down.
These guys, though, prayed and sang hymns
Till a thundering earthquake unlocked every door
And unleashed every prisoner within.

The jailer outside was scared for his life,
But Paul shouted, "We didn't flee!"
Then the jailer's whole family was baptized in faith,
While Silas and Paul were set free.

⊃ **Acts 16:16–40**

When mean people
need help, share
your best stuff.
They'll feel like jerks,
and God will reward
you for being kind.
Proverbs 25:21–22

BLIND RAGE

Once the strongest man on earth,
Samson had been dumb.
He'd told an evil woman where
His superstrength came from.

He'd made a vow about his hair
To not cut it at all.
But trusting his strength more than God
Caused silly Samson's fall.

He'd told Delilah two big lies
Of how to steal his might.
And though she'd tried to have him killed,
He shared the truth one night.

Delilah then called in some men,
And they shaved Samson's head.
They tied him up and taunted him,
For all his strength had fled.

They shackled him with chains of bronze.
They gouged out Samson's eyes.
A prisoner, they made him toil
And laughed at Samson's cries.

One day they had a party planned
To worship their fake god,
So they brought blind Samson in
To entertain the crowd.

They didn't notice then at all
That he had hair again.
But Samson did and prayed to God,
"Please strengthen me. Amen."

And pushing on two columns tall
That held the building's roof,
Samson brought the whole place down.
Of God his strength was proof.

➲ **Judges 16:4–30**

BIG MAN, BIG MOUTH, BIG FALL

The Israelite army was trembling
At the sight of the enemy force,
Especially the giant Goliath,
Who shook their camp with his roars.

"Come out and face me!" he challenged.
"I dare you to send just one man!
Whichever of us kills the other
Will win this war for his clan."

But Goliath was nine feet of tallness,
With armor both heavy and thick.
His spear was as long as a flagpole,
And his legs were as solid as brick.

The Israelites all were too frightened
To face that monstrous giant,
Until a young shepherd named David
Said, "On God we must be reliant."

When King Saul heard about David,
He called the youngster to him.
"Do you want to fight 'gainst this giant?
You'll surely be torn limb from limb."

"Not true," answered David quite calmly.
"See, I've killed both lions and bears,
And likewise this scumbag will perish,
For God will answer our prayers."

Saul tried to give David his armor,
But that and Saul's sword just felt odd.
So David instead put his trust in
His slingshot, five stones, and his God.

"Do you think I'm a dog?" yelled Goliath.
"Your flesh I will feed to each bird!"
But David floored him with a stone throw
And chopped off his head with a sword.

⮑ 1 Samuel 17:1–51

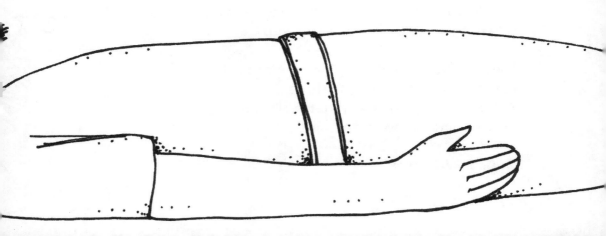

A SHIPWRECK AND A SNAKEBITE

Paul had seen many dangers and scares
In his work of preaching God's Word.
So when he was jailed and sent off to Rome,
Paul placed his full trust in the Lord.

The boat that held Paul and his fellow jailbirds
Was battered around by a squall.
The seawater bashed Paul's ship back and forth,
And they tossed all supplies they could haul.

With little food left and even less hope,
The men were expecting the end.
Paul stood up just then and said, "Men, be brave.
God has promised our lives to defend."

The ship struck a reef, and death seemed at hand,
But they all made it safely to shore.
Topping it off, when a snake bit Paul's hand,
He lived and was not even sore.

➲ **Acts 27:1–28:5**

Like stormy skies without rain is a kid who promises gifts but then doesn't give them.
Proverbs 25:14

ALL FIRED UP

Nebuchadnezzar, an arrogant king,
Made a statue ninety feet tall.
And he commanded when music was played,
In worship all people must fall.

"Pray to my idol," ordered the king,
"Or I'll give you more than a stern face.
Those who refuse to worship will be
Thrown into a fiery furnace."

Horns and pipes played, and people bowed down.
Three youths, though, refused this great sin.
King Nebuchadnezzar screamed his head off,
"Bow down, or to fire go in!"

Abednego, Shadrach, and Meshach, the three,
Said, "God has the power to save.
But even if He lets us burn in the flames,
We won't do this bad thing you crave."

"Crank the blaze up to the max!" yelled the king.
"Then pitch these dumb fools in the fire!"
The three were tossed in, but those who threw them
From the heat did in death expire.

The craziest part is what King Neb saw next.
The three young guys didn't look dead.
The king could see walking around in the fire
Four men who looked happy instead.

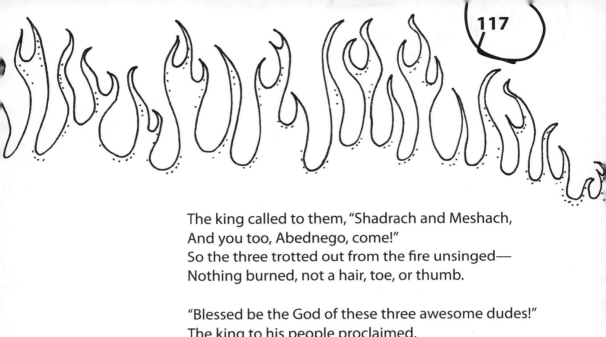

The king called to them, "Shadrach and Meshach,
And you too, Abednego, come!"
So the three trotted out from the fire unsinged—
Nothing burned, not a hair, toe, or thumb.

"Blessed be the God of these three awesome dudes!"
The king to his people proclaimed.
"I tried to turn them into crispy-fried guys,
But their God these fires have tamed."

➲ **Daniel 3**

THE DANGERS OF LONG HAIR

Years after Goliath
Was killed by that sling,
Shepherd David had grown
To be Israel's king.

Now Absalom was
A son of King Dave
Who hated his father
And his throne did crave.

A proud, handsome man
With long, flowing hair,
Absalom and his army
Had caused much despair.

Absalom rode out
On a mule swiftly
And was caught by his hair
In the branch of a tree.

He hung there, quite stuck,
Till Dave's general came by,
Who thrice javelined him—
What a bad way to die!

➲ **2 Samuel 18:1–15**

HORSEMEN, A DRAGON, AN EARTHQUAKE, AND DEATH!

The final book of Bible truth
Is strange and hard to get.
It's filled with symbols, signs, and words
About what's coming yet.

The smartest minds in all the world
Don't know what each line means,
But there's lots of scary stuff
In these prophetic scenes.

Four horse riders—one named Death—
Kill lots with plague and sword.
An earthquake blackens out the sun,
And blood and fire are poured.

Insect horses, beasts, a dragon
Do great evil then.
Don't fear, though, for God's dear Lamb
Will win and say, "Amen!"

➲ **Revelation 6; 8–9; 12–13; 16–17; 20–22**

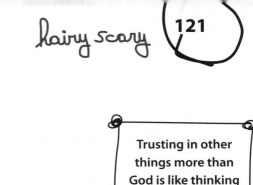

Trusting in other things more than God is like thinking a scarecrow can chase after bunnies in a garden.
Jeremiah 10:5

HOT LIPS

In his work as a prophet,
Isaiah preached much
Of repenting and trusting,
Of waiting and such.

But the most wonderful
And most terrible sight
Was his vision of God
And His angels in flight.

Six wings had each angel
Who shouted God's praise,
While the foundations shook
And thick smoke did raise.

"Woe is me," said Isaiah,
"For my lips are unclean.
And I am not worthy
To see what I've seen."

Then one of the angels
With tongs swiftly grabbed
A hot, burning coal,
And with it he jabbed.

He touched that coal to
Isaiah's shocked lips.
He said, "You're clean now.
This coal your sin strips."

The voice of God rumbled,
"Whom shall I send out?"
"Here am I! Send me!"
Was Isaiah's bold shout.

Through him God would share
Both judgment and woe,
But also His promise
Of a Savior would grow.

⊃ **Isaiah 6**

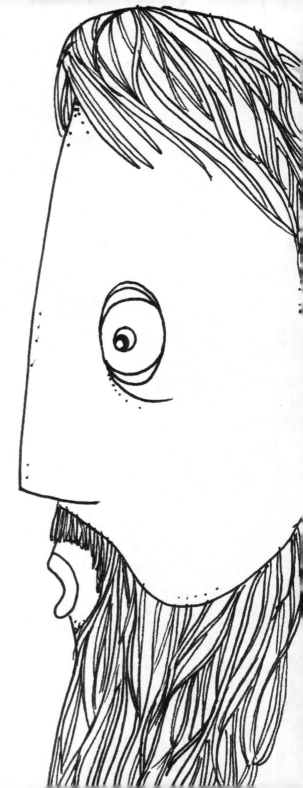

A HAIRY SCARY OBITUARY

Billions and billions of terrible things—
Fierce monsters and bullies and wars—
Are lurking each night right under our beds,
Within walls, and outside our doors.

We're scared these giants and fires and beasts
Will burn us and rip us apart,
'Cause we feel so small, and they're crazy huge,
That we don't even know where to start.

Should we sling small stones or grow out our hair,
Build an ark or a snake on a stick?
Maybe a donkey will show us the way
Or the sea waves will part super quick?

God loves to make miracles happen—it's true!
But the wonder that He loves the best
Is giving us faith in Jesus, His Son,
Who smacks down death and the rest!

So take that, you lions! You snakes have no bite!
Lightning and quakes may lash out,
But God says, "Just pray, and you cannot lose.
Christ wins, hands down! Have no doubt!"

➲ **1 Corinthians 15:54–57; Ephesians 6:10–18**

BIBLE STORY INDEX

Icky Sticky Stories

Hairy Scary Stories

Wise Sayings

ABOUT THE AUTHOR

Jonathan Schkade (pronounced "Skah-dee," rhymes with "body") lives in the village of Hamel, Illinois, with his sparkling wife, Kristi, and their sweet little daughter. Despite his best efforts, Jonathan graduated from Concordia University in Seward, Nebraska, with a degree in elementary education and a major in procrastination.

He's published five books, including *Icky Sticky, Hairy Scary Bible Stories* and *The Father's Easter Story,* and has written for day school curriculum, *Happy Times* magazine, *My Devotions,* and *Portals of Prayer.* While getting himself into and out of messes in his books fills up most of his time, he also loves singing in his church's choir, eating Tater Tots, playing as many board games as possible, and daydreaming for fun and profit.

ABOUT THE ARTIST

Tuesday Mourning grew up in Colorado, where she and her eight brothers and sisters drew constantly. She looked forward to rainy days as they meant a lot of time indoors drawing paper dolls with her sisters and creating elaborate stories about them. She later received her Bachelor's of Fine Art at Brigham Young University, where she learned how to draw and paint for a living. Tuesday currently resides in Southern California with her husband and two sons.

Tuesday has illustrated the covers of over twenty chapter books, including Paula Danziger's *The Cat Ate My Gymsuit* and Elizabeth Cody Kimmel's *Suddenly Supernatural* series, and has illustrated several picture books, including Pam Calvert's popular *Princess Peepers* and Eve Feldman's acclaimed *Billy and Milly, Short and Silly.*